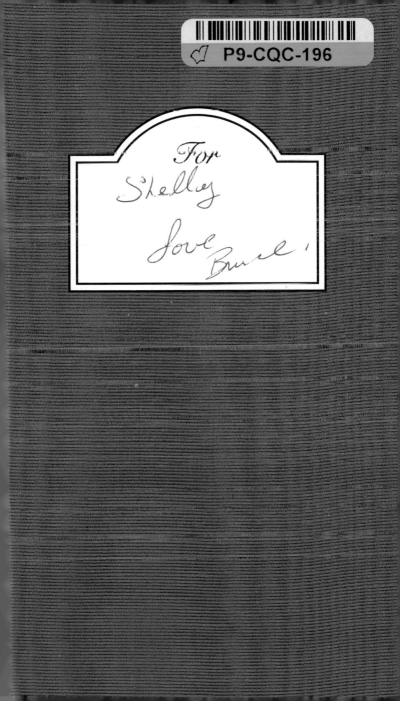

For
Shelley

love
Bruce

Mothers

&

Daughters

That Special Bond

Edited by
Suzanne Beilenson

Design by
Barbara Cohen Aronica
and Arlene Greco

PETER PAUPER PRESS, INC.
WHITE PLAINS, NEW YORK

For my own wonderful mother,

Evelyn Loeb Beilenson

All photographs courtesy of UPI/Bettmann except
Reuters/Bettmann p. 35, The Bettmann Archive
p. 53, and UPI/Bettmann Newsphotos pp. 6, 24.

Contents

Introduction

*A*t any given moment, she is your best friend, your closest confidante, your mirror image, or even the bane of your existence. No matter what, though, she is always the most important woman in your life. She is your mother. She is your daughter.

*T*here is no other relationship quite as special as the one between a mother and her daughter. A daughter learns her first lessons at her mother's knee. As a girl grows, her mother is her role model for becoming a woman. She will imitate that image, co-opt that image, and maybe even rebel against it, but it is always her mother who defines the standard.

*L*ikewise, a mother learns just as much from her daughter. She sees the best of herself in her daughter, and sometimes the not-so-best. A mother

always has hopes and dreams for her
daughter. Yet, in growing up, a daughter's life can
fulfill those ideals or simply baffle her mother.
Always, though, a daughter opens new horizons for
her mother, shows her the unending possibilities of
the world, the changes that come with the times,
and new definitions of being a woman.

*A*s you'll see from the quotations in this book, the
bond between a mother and daughter is one of the
strongest in each of their lives. The love between
them is a rock in the often turbulent waters of life.
They are women standing together—learning, living,
and, most of all, loving.

S.B.

Rita Hayworth and daughter Princess Yasmin Khan

From

the Bottom

Looking Up:

Daughters Talk

About Their

Mothers

*I*n search of my mother's garden I found my own.

ALICE WALKER

*T*wo years ago, a friend commented to me
about how many lists I made and how many
little yellow stick-'ems I leave around the
house to remind myself of things. At that moment it
dawned on me that I had become . . . Joan Rivers!

MELISSA RIVERS

I didn't run away. I haven't been kidnapped. I'm out
at the clubs. You can punish me in the morning.

GWYNETH PALTROW,
NOTE ON HER PILLOW

*M*y mother wanted me to be her wings, to fly
as she never quite had the courage to do.

ERICA JONG

*M*om used to be very reckless and irresponsible.
Now she's more mature.

MOLLY JONG-FAST

*M*other showed me and the world that no matter where you are born, to whom and under what conditions, you can achieve anything you want. She walked with kings, queens and presidents and never lost the human touch.

DEE DEE BELLSON,
DAUGHTER OF PEARL BAILEY

I'm able to write about a good mother because I had a good mother—unequivocally. She was quite different than I am . . . I'm a somewhat driven, ambitious person, very interested in an intellectual life. My mother wasn't like that. She was quieter and more reserved than I am. . . . She had a vested interest in making us feel good. At the time, I took it for granted that that's how mothers were, and now I just thank God almost every day.

ANNA QUINDLEN

I often think of my mother. Though I do not remember what she looked like, I feel her presence with me all the time. I still feel her warmth, her beauty . . .

EARTHA KITT

Mama exhorted her children at every opportunity to "jump at de sun." We might not land on the sun, but at least we would get off the ground.

ZORA NEALE HURSTON

It was difficult growing up the child of a famous mother. I didn't like what I saw: managers, lawyers. . . . From seeing Mom's life, I knew what I didn't want for mine.

TAHNEE WELCH

Jacqueline Kennedy Onassis and daughter Caroline

*W*hen Jimmy Carter was President, he called and said, "Loretta, we want you to come up here. Five famous people will come in and bring the teacher that has taught 'em the most." . . . So I told President Carter I couldn't bring a teacher. And he said, "Why?" I said, "Well, my mommy was what taught me most." And he said, "Well, there's always got to be a first. Bring her." That was the biggest thrill that my mother ever had.

LORETTA LYNN

*M*om can really tell a story, and she liked to lay it on real thick. She can be very dramatic. She knew how to wring us dry—and she had the goods. We'd sit around her and listen, and then we would start to sob and sniffle and say, "Mommy, you had the worst life. We'll be good to you, we will, we will." Sometimes I thought maybe she did that to control us, to make us be a little sweeter. But I don't think so. She's not that devious. But it had that effect anyhow.

KATHIE LEE GIFFORD

I was supposed to be just like her; I was supposed to fight with everyone to prove that I was one of the strong ones too.

B. D. HYMAN,
ON HER MOTHER, BETTE DAVIS

*A*lthough my mother and I were nothing alike, I realized that I was her girl more than I had ever been my father's. She had made me stand out from other girls, had dressed me, had taught me to sing, had let me quit school. And now she was encouraging me to grow up . . .

GLORIA SWANSON

*F*or years, I couldn't admit that my mother was an alcoholic. Our family kept the problem hushed up, as families did in those days. But in time, the roles of Mother and myself were reversed: I became the mother, taking care of her, undressing her and putting her to bed. . . . It was a difficult life, but perhaps coping with Mother strengthened me. Perhaps it was something like being in the Marines, in boot camp: once you went through it, you were ready for anything. Griping and self-pity got you nowhere.

HELEN HAYES

*S*he is the parent I remember and hers is the life I keep mining for gold, running my sieve through the same old streams, searching for precious nuggets that might connect my memories of her to the life I have lived without her. I keep hoping that the missing pieces will turn up in my mother's past.

LETTY COTTIN POGREBIN

I never would've treated a friend [so badly]. But she was my mother. I knew that no matter what I did or said, she'd come back, hoping for a change of heart. It got to the point where I'd reduce her to tears. "I love you," she'd plead. "Why are you doing this to me? To us?" I didn't know what to say.

DREW BARRYMORE

*M*amma from the beginning came one week of each month to be with us. It was marvelous! And Christmas! And half of each summer we were with her. When she was with us, her time was entirely ours. She never went out to dinner or had a friend to visit. She was totally ours.

ISABELLA ROSSELLINI

*F*or me, the most personal thing I ever said on the air had to do with my mother, who had recently died. I said that she'd wanted to go to college but there was no money, that she'd wanted to work but her husband wouldn't let her, that she'd wanted to go into politics but she knew no other women in politics. She'd said it wasn't her time. Instead, she'd pushed me to read, to stretch . . . She said it was my time . . .

LINDA ELLERBEE

*M*other came from a self-supporting family, where work was work and play was work. If any of us weren't good at what we were being taught (as I wasn't at painting), those lessons ended. Her overwhelming belief in us didn't blind her. . . . and that's probably one very good reason why I was able to become what I became.

SUZANNE FARRELL

*M*y sister said once: "Anything I don't want Mother to know, I don't even *think* of, if she's in the room."

AGATHA CHRISTIE

My mother is always looking for bargains. Excruciating for a child to watch her mother fight off other women for a dress, even if it is for me. Dressing rooms like stalls for animals. Women behaving like animals. Store employees treating them like animals. It creates in me a desire to buy retail for the rest of my life.

JULIA PHILLIPS

There is a point where you aren't as much mom and daughter as you are adults and friends. It doesn't happen for everyone—but it did for Mom and me.

JAMIE LEE CURTIS

Always I heard Mother's emotional voice asking Amy and me and our younger sister, Molly, the same few questions: Is that your own idea? Or somebody else's? She was scathingly sarcastic about the McCarthy hearings and she frantically opposed Father's usual wait-and-see calm. She herself held many unpopular, even fantastic, positions. Opposition emboldened her, and she would take on anybody on any issue.

ANNIE DILLARD

*A*fter she married a musician, Momma learned how to play guitar from him, and with the help of more books, taught herself to read music and understand music theory. After a while, she knew as much as a college music student did. She knew enough to teach somebody else the basics. I was one of her first pupils.

BARBARA MANDRELL

She's my teacher, my adviser, my greatest inspiration.

WHITNEY HOUSTON

*M*omma was home. She was the most totally human, human being that I have ever known; and so very beautiful. She was the lighthouse of her community. Within our home, she was an abundance of love, discipline, fun, affection, strength, tenderness, encouragement, understanding, inspiration, support.

LEONTYNE PRICE

I hear my mother when I'm being my best self—
soothing someone else. . . . My mother's big message
was that you take care of other people—whether it's
the city of New Orleans, the Democratic party or a
little mutt from the pound.

COKIE ROBERTS

*O*ne of my earliest memories is of my mother
. . . setting aside dollars for the specific charity
requests that touched them. She taught me that I
had an obligation to give something back to society,
no matter how little that could be some months.

ALI MCGRAW

*T*he first time I realized I had become my mother
was when I moved into my new apartment. It has
this amazing, fully equipped kitchen—and I ordered
in Chinese food. I'm the worst cook ever—just like
my mother.

RICKI LAKE

*W*hen my mother had to get dinner for eight she'd
just make enough for sixteen and only serve half.

GRACIE ALLEN

I couldn't have a better friend than my mother. I never had to be afraid to talk to her about anything. . . . And the basic things that my mother taught me are pretty much right on. But she never restricted me. . . . If I wanted to do something that she didn't approve of she'd say, "Well, I usually tell you how it is. If you want to go ahead and do this, it's up to you. But just know that I don't approve."

LACY J. DALTON

Cher holding daughter Chastity.
Cher's mother, Georgia Holt, is at left.

*I*t was no great tragedy being Judy Garland's daughter. I had tremendously interesting childhood years—except they had little to do with being a child.

LIZA MINNELLI

*M*y mom buys things I wouldn't wear in a million years.

CHASTITY BONO,
DAUGHTER OF CHER

*W*hen my mom got really mad, she would say, "Your butt is my meat." Not a particularly attractive phrase. And I always wondered, "Now, what wine goes with that?"

PAULA POUNDSTONE

I don't blame the daughter, don't blame her at all for writing *Mommie Dearest*. . . . I doubt she could have written this if it weren't true. One area of life Joan should never have gotten into was children. She bought them.

BETTE DAVIS,
ON JOAN CRAWFORD

*F*aye Dunaway says she is being haunted by mother's ghost. After her performance in *Mommie Dearest*, I can understand why.

CHRISTINA CRAWFORD

*S*he had curiosity and enthusiasm for anything new. And she stood behind me all the way. If I wanted to be a dancer, an actress—that was what I would be if there was anything she could do about it.

LAUREN BACALL,
ON HER MOTHER

*W*henever I'm with my mother, I feel as though I have to spend the whole time avoiding land mines.

AMY TAN

*F*rom the time I was a child I wanted to be like my mother. Not necessarily an actress—I never dreamed I'd have the courage—but an active, volatile woman like she was.

ISABELLA ROSSELLINI

I have a feeling we'll get closer as I grow older and have kids of my own. Grandchildren will be such a bond—especially when I'll need a baby-sitter!

SUZANNE KAY,
DAUGHTER OF DIAHANN CARROLL

*M*y mother looked to me like a fairy princess, far too beautiful to be a Mom—a fair, rare creature who lived in a magic kingdom. I always entered her dressing room as if drawn into a dream. Her domain was draped in ice-blue taffeta sprinkled with violets and sparkled with antique silver, Venetian glass, and tiny enameled boxes. Only a princess belonged here, not a six-year-old with clumsy hands.

CANDICE BERGEN

*T*here was a hemlock tree on the west side of the property. That was the tree I used to climb. The neighbors used to call Mother. "Kit! Kathy is in the top of the hemlock!" "Yes, I know. Don't scare her. She doesn't know that it's dangerous."

KATHARINE HEPBURN

*M*y mother wouldn't let me watch *The Donna Reed Show*. She hated it. She didn't have a washer or dryer, and we didn't even have a furnace until I was in high school.

NAOMI JUDD

*W*hen we weren't scratching each other's eyes out, we were making each other laugh harder than anyone else could.

LUCIE ARNAZ,
WORKING WITH HER MOTHER ON
I LOVE LUCY

*"A*nd I mean it!"* is the phrase my mother used when she really wanted me to do something. Now I tell my daughter Ellie, "Get out of the bathtub—*and I mean it!"* The other day, I overheard Ellie [age 2-1/2] in the playground, bossing around the other little kids: *"And I mean it!"*

KATIE COURIC

*M*y mother was always working—a concert, an album, a movie, a television show. She taught Liza (Minnelli) and me to enjoy what we do. When I told her I wanted to go into this industry, the best advice she gave me was to study. "You're not going to make it on my name," she said.

LORNA LUFT

I feel about mothers the way I feel about dimples: because I do not have one myself, I notice everyone who does.

LETTY COTTIN POGREBIN

I really am the complete extrovert and I always have been—my mother says that I used to wink at people when I was in my pram.

ESTHER RANTZEN

*M*y mother told me I was dancing before I was born. She could feel my toes tapping wildly inside her for months.

GINGER ROGERS

*W*hen Mother turned 80, I threw a birthday party. More than 70 people came, my generation and hers, friends and cronies from way back. The celebration started at three in the afternoon because I was sure that Mother and the other old girls would tire early. I should have known better.

MARY HIGGINS CLARK

"*M*ama, Mama," I said happily, "I think I've met a man I could marry." My mother was ecstatic—at first; I was, after all, twenty-six years old and in Jewish families mothers have long since begun to despair when their babies reach that age unmarried. "There's a small problem . . . He's still married. . . . He has three children, he's thirteen years older than I, and he's not Jewish." Mama burst into tears: "Why does everything have to happen to my baby?"

BEVERLY SILLS

Priscilla Presley and daughter Lisa Marie

*M*y mother was very strong. She wouldn't give me money. If I wanted something I earned it. . . . If I got A's, she said, "Why not A+'s." If I got A+'s, it was, "It's not a hard school." My mother's responsible for my drive. I've always had drive.

JUDITH REGAN

*N*ow that I am in my forties, she tells me I'm beautiful; now that I am in my forties, she sends me presents and we have the long, personal and even remarkably honest phone calls I always wanted so intensely I forbade myself to imagine them. How strange. . . . I am deeply grateful. With my poems, I finally won even my mother. The longest wooing of my life.

MARGE PIERCY

*W*hen Mother taught us the Lord's Prayer, she put her heart into it. You tried to say it as she did, and you had to put a little of your own heart into it. I believe that Mother, realizing that she was left alone to raise three girls, knew that she had to have a support beyond herself.

MARIAN ANDERSON

*W*hen I first started entertainin', Mama would say, "Now, Reba, your jokes are real cute, but just quit talkin' and sing. . . . God put me on this earth to sing. Basically He gave the voice first to Mama. But Mama couldn't use it, so she passed it down to us kids. So that's how it worked out.

REBA MCENTIRE

*M*y mother was filled with passionate resentment about the condition of women, as perhaps my grandmother might have been had my grandfather lived and had she borne five children and had little opportunity to use her special gifts and training. As it was, the two women I knew best were mothers and had professional training. So I had no reason to doubt that brains were suitable for a woman.

MARGARET MEAD

*M*y mother taught me to forget past hurts—ex-husbands, people who've hurt your feelings. "You should forgive and forget," she said. "Move on." Her favorite expression was, "Have good health and a bad memory."

PIA LINDSTROM

My mother used to have an expression: "There's only one woman around this house—and it's me!"

NAOMI CAMPBELL

No matter how perfect your mother thinks you are, she will always want to fix your hair.

SUZANNE BEILENSON

I am Lena's daughter. My daughters are her grand-daughters. Family faces are magic mirrors. Looking at people who belong to us, we see the past, present, and future.

GAIL HORNE JONES LUMET

I could not hide from myself that she was doomed, and I tried to face a world in which I could never see her face again. I had learned to live my own life and yet it was rooted in my deep relationship with her. The relationship was sometimes irksome because . . . I loved her so well and understood her and recognized in myself certain qualities which were hers.

PEARL S. BUCK

*M*y mother had a problem because she grew up during the Great Depression. And I had problems because I grew up during *her* great depression.

JANE STROLL

*E*ven when [my mother]'s performing her favorite act of relaxation—which is spearing slimy garden slugs with toothpicks—she wears her Maud Frizon shoes.

LINDA FRUM

*A*nd for the three magic gifts I needed to escape the poverty of my hometown, I thank my mother, who gave me a sewing machine, a typewriter, and a suitcase. . . .

ALICE WALKER

*T*o describe my mother would be to write about a hurricane in its perfect power. Or the climbing, falling colors of a rainbow.

MAYA ANGELOU

I remember sitting in the corner when I was a little girl, listening as my mother taught elocution. After her student left, I repeated the piece they had been working on, word for word. I also remember my mother telling me that she had named me Jane (there had been several Janes in her mother's family) because she could see *Jane Russell* looking good in lights.

JANE RUSSELL

*M*y mother wanted me to be a star and I worked hard for her goal.

LENA HORNE

I used to be so bad I had a curfew of noon. . . .
To sneak out at night I would creep down the stairs between our two golden retrievers. When I passed my mother's door—her hearing is acute—I used to jangle their chains so she would think it was the dogs.

GWYNETH PALTROW

*A*s the only girl, I was guarded with the vigor of a dragon-slaying St. George. Mother felt it was her duty to see that I came unscathed through the dating years. Whenever I walked up the block with a date, no matter the hour, she would be at the window. I'd groan inwardly and wait for the familiar call "Is that you, Mary?" I'd want to reply, "No, it's Gunga Din." But her method was effective. No suitor ever got fresh, with that alert sentry dangling 20 feet above his head.

MARY HIGGINS CLARK

*T*he first time I heard my mother's voice come out of my mouth was when I started yelling at my sisters, "Clean up after yourselves!" It's something my mother said—and now I can't help but say it too.

CHRISTY TURLINGTON

*M*y mother raised me to be independent— as she is. Hitchcock gave her an ultimatum: go to bed with him or he'd ruin her career. "Ruin it," Mom said.

MELANIE GRIFFITH

Vanessa Redgrave and daughter Natasha Richardson

I wasn't allowed to have pictures of movie stars on my bedroom walls. I started to act in college, and I couldn't give it up. But I was nervous about it socially. To this day, my mother hasn't seen much of my work. She's still not comfortable with the notion of acting.

STOCKARD CHANNING

I don't put her in the same category with Candice Bergen or Cher or any of those, but I guess she is. It's hard for me to believe.

PATTY MICCI,
DAUGHTER OF CYBILL SHEPHERD

I always wanted a mother who was fat and stayed home and baked cookies all the time, someone who made you feel safe so that when something bad happened to you, you could come home and hide behind her. Instead, I had a cool mother, who wore miniskirts and went to nightclubs, and a dad I don't know much anymore.

PAULINA PORIZKOVA

*M*y mother was the mother of the world. She'd correct people's manners and morals without even knowing them. It wasn't until I grew up that I really understood how great a woman she was—her high standards, strict discipline, good manners, work habits. I learned from her that when you mop a floor, you get down on your hands and knees to get into the corners.

DEE DEE BELLSON,
DAUGHTER OF PEARL BAILEY

I was rebelling against being Carol Burnett's daughter. When I was stoned, I felt better about myself. Drugs became a perfect way for Carrie Hamilton to exist as herself.

CARRIE HAMILTON

*M*y mother told me stories all the time . . . And in all of those stories she told me who I was, who I was supposed to be, whom I came from, and who would follow me. In this way, she taught me the meaning of the words she said, that all life is a circle and everything has a place within it.

PAULA GUNN ALLEN

*W*hen I was a teen [my mother] refused to get a hair dryer, and for years my sister and I had to dry our hair in front of the electric heater.

LIONA BOYD

*A*nd it came to me, and I knew what I had to have before my soul would rest. I wanted to belong—to belong to my mother. And in return—I wanted my mother to belong to me.

GLORIA VANDERBILT

I miss thee, my Mother! Thy image is still
The deepest impressed on my heart.

ELIZA COOK

*D*ear Mother: I'm all right. Stop worrying about me.

*PAPYRUS LETTER OF 17-YEAR-OLD
EGYPTIAN GIRL, CA. 2000 B.C.*

Whoopi Goldberg and daughter Alex

From the Top

Looking Down:

What Mothers

Say About

Their

Daughters

*M*y daughter's birth was the incomparable gift of seeing the world at quite a different angle than before, and judging it by standards that would apply far beyond my natural life.

ALICE WALKER

I could tell that night that Cher was going to be a star. When a person has that incredible presence, it's just a question of time.

GEORGIA HOLT,
CHER'S MOTHER

*T*hey're all mine. . . . Of course, I'd trade any one of them for a dishwasher.

ROSEANNE,
THE TV ROSEANNE, ABOUT HER CHILDREN

*T*oday's mothers have certain values, hard-won, in common. Primary is the conviction that their daughters must be defined from the inside out as opposed to the reverse.

PHYLLIS THEROUX

I love my daughter. She and I have shared my body. There is a part of her mind that is a part of mine. But when she was born, she sprang from me like a slippery fish, and has been swimming away ever since.

AMY TAN

I think it is important to convey to my daughter, who is five, a sense of possibilities about her place in the world. We've taught her to aspire to life in a world that is gender-neutral, and at the same time have encouraged her to challenge things not in keeping with that vision.

SUSAN G. COLE

*W*atching Clementine grow is one of the great satisfactions of my life. The center of the universe shifting from myself to another person is a great relief. It gives me the chance to give to another person. I'm not so concerned about my own life as I was before.

CYBILL SHEPHERD

I was not a classic mother. But my kids were never palmed off to boarding school. So I didn't bake cookies. You can buy cookies, but you can't buy love.

RAQUEL WELCH

I never want [my daughters] to see me as a victim. It's important for me that they see that whether I win or lose, I can always stand up for what I believe.

ESTHER SHAPIRO

Lucille Ball and daughter Lucie Arnaz

As I look back on my early years of parenthood, one thing I regret is the amount of time I spent looking ahead toward my children's next big step. When they were born, I waited for them to smile. When they smiled, I watched for them to sit up. Not that I didn't take pleasure in the moment. But so much of raising children is about forward movement and growth. And, especially with a first child, . . . you know so little of the road ahead that you're always anticipating what's around the corner.

JOYCE MAYNARD

What I celebrate about my daughter is her frankness, her feistiness, her twin abilities to have her eyes flood with tears and apply eyeliner far better than I ever did.

PHYLLIS THEROUX

I knew what was important for me and that a successful career would mean nothing without a personal life. So the children would always be with me.

JANET LEIGH

*T*here has been no more profound reading experience in her 15 years than getting through *Hop on Pop* all by herself. . . . I can still hear her, lying alone in the semidarkness, repeating those thrilling words to herself long past the hour when I'd tucked her in and kissed her goodnight . . .

JOYCE MAYNARD

*N*obody's come beating down my door telling me I'm a terrible hussy. It didn't faze anybody—except Dan Quayle.

CATHERINE OXENBERG,
ON BEING A SINGLE MOTHER TO DAUGHTER INDIA

*T*he transmission of feminist values in our household has been a two-way path. While I have provided a model of independence, my daughter Kim has committed herself more systematically to the feminist movement—and raised my own awareness in the process.

SHIRLEY GOLDBERG

Debbie Reynolds holding daughter Carrie Fisher. Debbie's mother, Mrs. Maxene Reynolds is at left; her grandmother, Mrs. Maxene Harmon, is at right.

*M*elissa is the one to whom I could give total affection and feel it being absorbed and returned.

JOAN RIVERS

I have always felt guilty because for me work was important. My children know I love them . . . but I wonder if they resented my not being there all the time.

INGRID BERGMAN

I do not think I have been so much successful in communicating "feminist principles and conscious-ness" as in creating a space for my daughter, now ten years old, to be herself. Space to be who we are, space to grow in, spaces to be safe in—these are still not givens for women in today's society . . .

M. NOURBESE PHILIP

*I*t had long been the custom in our family that whenever one of us was sick or upset, the other would stay in bed until sleep came. Mom sometimes did this as well, and Natalie and I have done it with our daughters also.

LANA WOOD,
NATALIE WOOD'S SISTER

*I*t's such a shock when your child turns into a wild thing. When you've had a storybook child, and all of a sudden, you get the Exorcist. You walk in the room and see a green face with a tongue sticking out, say-ing, "I hate you!"

LEE GRANT

*G*wynnie is her own person. When we talk, I feel as if I've been invited to a secret place of hers. It makes those times that were difficult worthwhile.

BLYTHE DANNER

We are together, my child and I, Mother and child, yes, but sisters really, against whatever denies us all that we are.

ALICE WALKER

*A*s a parent, you stick your head in the sand, refusing to see, to apprehend what's right before your eyes. Carrie and I want the book to show what happens in the life of a family when you're afraid to confront your own child. . . . Today, if I'm upset, if I feel sad, if I feel mad at them, I let my daughters know it. I'm not afraid of the consequences any longer.

CAROL BURNETT

*T*o me, that isn't Paulina in those pictures and on the screen. I mean, to me, she's just my daughter.

ANNA PORIZKOVA

*I*n California, you work out your aggressions on the freeways because you spend so much time staying cool in the living rooms. When my daughter was three years old, she got into the swing of it by leaning out the car window and yelling, "If you can't drive it, park it!"

CYRA MCFADDEN

I never thought that I was very maternal but I just loved Melanie so much and enjoyed being with her. She's so happy now—and I'm so happy for her.

TIPPI HEDREN,
MELANIE GRIFFITH'S MOTHER

*R*emember you're loved.

LADY BIRD JOHNSON,
*ENDING CONVERSATIONS AND LETTERS
TO HER DAUGHTERS*

On the Inside

Looking Out:

Mothers and

Daughters in

Public Life

*Y*ou can't be the President of the United States and also be a mother.

BARBARA BUSH

*U*nlike most mothers, Mrs. Onassis did not interfere with Caroline's wedding dress design. In fact, she did not see the dress until it was finished. She said, "I am not going to get involved because Caroline is the one who will wear it. I want her to be the happiest girl in the world."

CAROLINA HERRERA

*M*y mother thought it's always a good idea not to buy things for people, but to either learn something from memory or do something with my hands. That has more value than something you buy.

CAROLINE KENNEDY

*M*y mother was strong and kind, but she was also free, a liberated woman, as was her mother before her, so it was inevitable that I would grow up to be vocal about women's issues.

BETTY FORD

I can still feel my mother's arms around me, holding me, as she stood out on the porch and we watched a storm come rolling in across the lake, waves swelling, thunder crashing, lightning slicing the sky, and my mother telling me how beautiful it was. I found out later she was scared to death, but she taught me not to be afraid; I was safe in those arms.

BETTY FORD

*M*other always said that I was supposed to be born on the Fourth of July, but the Yankees were playing a doubleheader that day (Mother was living in New York), and she was such a passionate baseball fan that she delayed my birth until July 6.

NANCY DAVIS REAGAN

*I*t makes perfect sense to me that given her upbringing, my mother wanted to become an actress. Acting is an escape; you can be someone else for a while, change reality. It's a sweet relief from whatever you don't want to look at in your own life.

PATTI DAVIS

I will probably never fully understand my mother's rage, because she edits her own history and reinvents it constantly. It is always a work in progress. The only consistencies in her stories are the things that contradict the person she is today. But there are pieces which, if fitted together carefully, start to form a picture.

PATTI DAVIS

*M*y mother died and created an emptiness so awful I thought my heart would burst. I kept wanting to talk to her, to explain, to ask, to remember. Suddenly, I realized that I missed my past life.

ELENA BONNER,
WIFE OF ANDREI SAKHAROV

*M*y darling Katya, my heart's blood, straight as a rowan tree, sweet as a cherry, what have I done to you?

SVETLANA ALLILUYEVA,
*STALIN'S DAUGHTER, AFTER DEFECTING,
TO HER DAUGHTER IN THE SOVIET UNION*

I pray that I may be all that [my mother] would have been, had she lived in an age when women could aspire and achieve.

RUTH BADER GINSBURG,
SUPREME COURT JUSTICE

*I*n character my mother is strict and demanding. I remember the scene when we accompanied my father off to the front. The overcrowded railway station—I really do recall from childhood so clearly and so sharply the railway stations with that unrepeatable sad atmosphere—women, children and tears. Many women even fainted. And I remember my mother, frozen in her grief. Her words were: "Who's going to support us? We must hold out."

RAISA GORBACHEV

*I*t was my mother, however, who taught me the rituals of prayer. She took her faith very seriously. No matter where she was in the world, or what she was doing, she prostrated herself five times a day in prayer. When I was nine years old, she began to include me, slipping into my bedroom to lead me in the morning prayer. Together we would perform the *wuzoo*, the washing of our hands, feet, and faces so that we would be pure before God, then prostrate ourselves facing west toward Mecca.

BENAZIR BHUTTO

I am not sure that Mother was always pleased with me. Often, before we came to [Israel] and afterward as well, when she would see me working hard and sometimes, as she thought, neglecting my home and my children, she would ask me: *"Goldah'le, vos vet zein die tachlis fun dir?"* ("What will be the end of you?") I am not sure if the end would have satisfied her.

GOLDA MEIR

From the Outside Looking In: Proverbs and Pundits on the Mother-Daughter Relationship

*B*ehold, every one that useth proverbs shall use
this proverb against thee, saying, As is the mother,
so is her daughter.

EZEKIEL 16:44-45

*W*hen a mother finally decides to give her daughter some advice, the mother usually learns plenty.

EVAN ESAR

Judy Garland and daughter Liza Minelli

*E*very one can keep House better than her Mother, till she trieth.

THOMAS FULLER

*M*other knows best—until daughter becomes a teen-ager.

EVAN ESAR

A light-heel'd mother makes a heavy heel'd daughter. Because she doth all the work herself, and her daughter the mean while sitting idle, contracts a habit of sloth.

JOHN RAY

*E*we follows ewe; as the acts of the mother, so are the acts of the daughter.

HEBREW PROVERB

*W*here do mothers learn all the things they tell their daughters not to do?

EVAN ESAR

*M*arry the daughter on knowing the mother.

HINDU PROVERB

*T*he daughter of a busy mother makes a bad housekeeper.

IRISH PROVERB

*T*he first child of a woman of good blood is always a girl.

ITALIAN PROVERB

*F*or a mother, sending your first child to college means learning to let go. I believe this is especially true when the child you're packing off is a daughter. The sense of identification is so much stronger than it is with a son. You can remember yourself as a young woman leaving home for school, the exhilaration and uncertainty of entering a new phase of life. But if going away to college is a rite of passage for a child, it is equally so for a mother.

JANE FONDA

I find it very heartening that of the women I have questioned lately about their feelings towards their mother, all the ones whose faces light up and say, "She's wonderful," have been daughters of women who work outside the home.

MARY STOTT

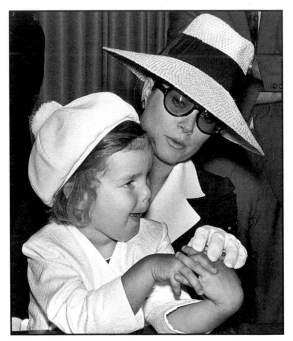

Princess Grace and daughter Princess Stephanie

Our mothers are our most direct connection to our history and our gender.

HOPE EDELMAN

*H*aving a bat and ball can be much less effective in encouraging a little girl to develop her physical aptitude than having a mother who jogs daily.

ARLENE EISENBERG, HEIDI E. M..........F, AND SANDEE E. ....AY

*P*uberty is when the boy you're crazy about calls and your mom gets to the phone first and starts asking questions. . . . Puberty is when all the other girls in class have bras whether they need them or not, but *your* mom says you're going to wait until you have a reason.

WILLIAM ALLEN

*W*hat *do* girls do who haven't any mothers to help them through their troubles?

LOUISA MAY ALCOTT

*C*all Your Mother—You've just found that nice Jewish boy she's always told you about. I live in . . .

PERSONAL AD

*W*hen a young girl begins to confide to her mother how silly it is for other young girls to pay any attention to boys, that is the time for her mother to look out for her own little girl.

REFLECTIONS OF A BACHELOR

*S*ometimes we blame Mom too much for all that is wrong with her sons and daughters. After all, we might well ask, who started the grim mess? Who long ago made Mom and her sex "inferior" and stripped her of her economic and political and sexual rights?

LILLIAN SMITH

*P*eople are just not very ambitious for women still. Your son you want to be the best you can. Your daughters you want to be happy.

ALEXA CANADY

*M*otherhood is *not* for the fainthearted. Used frogs, skinned knees, and the insults of teenage girls are not meant for the wimpy.

DANIELLE STEELE

*I*f a woman talks and acts as if her husband were just the provider for little Cindy, he can be forgiven for behaving as if she were just little Cindy's mother.

JOYCE BROTHERS

Former First Lady Betty Ford and daughter Susan

*A*cknowledging the tension, distance, and conflict, where is a map of the nurturance, the connection, the ways in which the torch is passed from mother to daughter or from daughter to mother?

COLETTE

*I*f women once learn to be something themselves, that the only way to teach is to be fine and shining examples, we will have in one generation the most remarkable and glorious children.

BRENDA VELAND

*W*ill your child learn to multiply before she learns to subtract?

CHILDREN'S DEFENSE FUND
ANTI-TEEN-PREGNANCY POSTER

*S*ome are kissing mothers and some are scolding mothers, but it is love just the same, and most mothers kiss and scold together.

PEARL S. BUCK

*M*other may I go and bathe?
Yes, my darling daughter.
Hang your clothes on yonder tree,
But don't go near the water.

NURSERY RHYME

*Y*oung women especially have something invested
in being *nice people,* and it's only when you have
children that you realize you're not a nice person at
all, but generally a selfish bully.

FAY WELDON

*T*he ultimate end of your education was to make
you a good wife.

LADY MARY WORTLEY MONTAGU

*M*y mother's hands are cool and fair,
They can do anything.
Delicate mercies hide them there
Like flowers in the spring.

ANNA HEMPSTEAD BRANCH

A fluent tongue is the only thing a mother don't like her daughter to resemble her in.

RICHARD BRINSLEY SHERIDAN

*D*aughter am I in my mother's house,
But mistress in my own.

RUDYARD KIPLING

*Y*ou never get over being a child, long as you have a mother to go to.

SARAH ORNE JEWETT

O more beautiful daughter of a beautiful mother.

HORACE

*T*he daughter begins to bloom before the mother can be content to fade, and neither can forbear to wish for the absence of the other.

SAMUEL JOHNSON

*A*s long as a woman can look ten years younger than her daughter she is perfectly satisfied.

OSCAR WILDE

*H*ow the mother is to be pitied who hath handsome daughters! Locks, bolts, bars, and lectures of morality are nothing to them: they break through them all. They have as much pleasure in cheating a father and mother, as in cheating at cards.

JOHN GAY,
THE BEGGAR'S OPERA

A lady with her daughters or her nieces
Shines like a guinea and seven-shilling pieces.

BYRON,
DON JUAN

*T*hou art thy mother's glass, and she in thee
Calls back the lovely April of her prime.

WILLIAM SHAKESPEARE,
SONNET